Tubbert 268-7909

P9-DFV-605

With Burning Hearts

With Burning Hearts

A Meditation on the Eucharistic Life

Henri J. M. Nouwen

ORBIS BOOKS

Maryknoll, New York 10545

Second Printing, September 1994

The Catholic Foreign Mission Society of America (Maryknoll) recruits and trains people for overseas missionary service. Through Orbis Books, Maryknoll aims to foster the international dialogue that is essential to mission. The books published, however, reflect the opinions of their authors and are not meant to represent the official position of the society.

Copyright © 1994 by Henri J. M. Nouwen

Published in the United States by Orbis Books,
Maryknoll, NY 10545-0308

All rights reserved. No part of this publication may be reproduced or transmitted in any form or by any means, electronic or mechanical, including photocopying, recording, or any information storage or retrieval system, without prior permission in writing from the publishers.

Excerpts from THE NEW JERUSALEM BIBLE, copyright © 1985 by Darton, Longman & Todd, Ltd. and Doubleday, a division of Bantam Doubleday Dell Publishing Group, Inc. Reprinted by Permission.

Manufactured in the United States of America

Library of Congress Cataloging-in-Publication Data
Nouwen, Henri J. M.
    With burning hearts : a meditation on the eucharistic life / Henri J. M. Nouwen.
    p.   cm.
    ISBN 0-88344-984-6
    1. Lord's Supper — Catholic Church — Meditations.   I. Title.
BX2169.N68   1994
234'.163–dc20   94-14622
                                                                      CIP

To Michael Harank
and all those who live and work
at Bethany House of Hospitality,
a Catholic Worker house in Oakland, California,
for homeless people living with AIDS

Contents

Acknowledgments

This book was written in Chobham, England and Sacramento, California. Bart and Patricia Gavigan offered me the lovely cottage at the Brookplace conference center, and Frank Hamilton let me use his cozy home at the Beale Air Force Base. I am deeply grateful to these special people, not only for understanding my need for a quiet space, but also, and even more so, for their supportive friendship.

Special thanks go to Kathy Christie and Conrad Wieczorek for their very competent secretarial and editorial help. To Sue Mosteller and Douglas Wiebe for their helpful comments on the first draft and to my editor, Robert Ellsberg, for his personal support, his many insightful suggestions, and his enthusiasm that helped me to bring this book to completion.

This book was written simply because I wanted to write it. Although nobody asked me, I had felt for a long time the urge to put down on paper thoughts and feelings about the Eucharist and the Eucharistic life that kept emerging in my mind and heart. As I started to present these thoughts and feelings

9

in lectures and conferences, I felt an increasing desire to put them in a small book to give to people in search of a spiritual life rooted in the Eucharist.

I hope that those who read this book will find here some new food and drink on their journey to God.

Introduction

Every day I celebrate the Eucharist. Sometimes in my parish church with hundreds of people present, sometimes in the Daybreak chapel with members of my community, sometimes in a hotel suite with a few friends, and sometimes in my father's living room with just him and me. Very few days pass without my saying, "Lord, have mercy," without the daily readings and a few reflections, without a profession of faith, without sharing the body and blood of Christ, and without a prayer for a fruitful day.

Still I wonder: Do I know what I am doing? Do those who stand or sit around the table with me know what they are part of? Does something really happen that shapes our daily lives — even though it is so familiar? And what about all those who are not there with us? Is the Eucharist still something they know about, think about, or desire? How is this daily celebration connected with the daily life of ordinary men and women, be they present or not? Is it more than a lovely ceremony, a soothing ritual, or a comfortable routine? And finally, does the Eucharist give life, life that has the power of overcoming death? All of these questions are very real to me; they constantly beg for an answer. Oh, yes, I have had answers, but it seems that they don't last very long in my quickly changing world. The Eucharist gives meaning to my being in the world, but as the world changes, does the Eucharist continue to give it meaning? I have read many books about the Eucharist. They were written ten, twenty, thirty, even forty years ago. Although they contain many deep insights, they no longer help me to experience the Eucharist as the center of my life. Today, the old questions are there again: How can all of my life be Eucharistic, and how can the daily celebration of the Eucharist make it that way? I have to come up with my own response. Without such a response, the Eucharist may become little more than a beautiful tradition.

This little book is an attempt to speak to myself and to my friends about the Eucharist and to weave a network of connections between the daily celebration of the Eucharist and our daily human experience. We enter every celebration with a contrite heart and pray the *Kyrie Eleison.* We listen to the Word — the scriptural readings and the homily — we profess our faith, we give to God the fruits of the earth and the work of human hands and receive from God the body and blood of Jesus, and finally we are sent into the world with the task of renewing the face of the earth. The Eucharistic event reveals the deepest human experiences, those of sadness, attentiveness, invitation, intimacy, and engagement. It summarizes the life we are called to live in the Name of God. Only when we recognize the rich network of connections between the Eucharist and our life in the world can the Eucharist be "worldly" and our life "Eucharistic."

As the basis for my reflections on the Eucharist and the Eucharistic life, I will use the story of the two disciples who walked from Jerusalem to Emmaus and back. As the story speaks about loss, presence, invitation, communion, and mission it embraces the five main aspects of the Eucharistic celebration.

Together they form a movement, the movement from resentment to gratitude, that is, from a hardened heart to a grateful heart. While the Eucharist expresses this spiritual movement in a very succinct way, the Eucharistic life is one in which we are invited to experience and affirm this movement in every moment of our daily existence. In this little book I hope to develop the five steps of this movement from resentment to gratitude in such a way that it becomes clear that what we celebrate and what we are called to live are essentially one and the same.

The Road
to Emmaus

N *ow that very same day, two of them were on their way to a village called Emmaus, seven miles from Jerusalem, and they were talking together about all that had happened. And it happened that as they were talking together and discussing it, Jesus himself came up and walked by their side; but their eyes were prevented from recognizing him. He said to them, "What are all these things that you are discussing as you walk along?" They stopped, their faces downcast.*

Then one of them, called Cleopas, answered him, "You must be the only person staying in Jerusalem who does not know the things that have been happening there these last few days." He asked, "What things?" They answered, "All about Jesus of Nazareth, who showed himself a prophet powerful in action and speech before God and the whole people; and how our chief priests and our leaders handed him over to be sentenced to death, and had him crucified. Our own hope had been that he would be the one to set Israel free. And this is not all; two whole days have now gone by since it all happened; and some women from our group have astounded us: they went to the tomb in the early morning, and when they could not find the body, they came back to tell us they had seen a vision of angels who declared he was alive. Some of our friends went to the tomb and found everything exactly as the women had reported, but of him they saw nothing."

Then he said to them, "You foolish men! So slow to believe all that the prophets have said! Was it not necessary that the Christ should suffer before entering into his glory?" Then, starting with Moses and going through all the prophets, he explained to them the passages throughout the scriptures that were about himself.

When they drew near to the village to which they were going, he made as if to go on; but they pressed him to stay with them saying, "It is nearly evening, and the day is almost over." So he went in to stay with them.

Now while he was with them at table, he took the bread and said the blessing; then he broke it and handed it to them. And their eyes were opened and they recognized him; but he had vanished from their sight. Then they said to each other, "Did not our hearts burn within us as he talked to us on the road and explained the scriptures to us?"

They set out that instant and returned to Jerusalem. There they found the Eleven assembled together with their companions, who said to them, "The Lord has indeed risen and has appeared to Simon." Then they told their story of what had happened on the road and how they had recognized him at the breaking of bread.

(Luke 24:13–35)

I

Mourning
Our Losses

"Lord, Have Mercy"

Two people are walking together. You can see from the way they walk that they are not happy. Their bodies are bent over, their faces are downcast, their movements slow. They do not look at each other. Once in a while they utter a word, but their words are not directed to each other. They vanish in the air as useless sounds. Although they follow the path on which they walk, they seem to have no goal. They return to their home, but their home is no longer home. They simply have no other place to go. Home has become emptiness, disillusionment, despair.

They can hardly imagine that it was only a few years ago when they had met someone who had changed their lives, someone who had radically interrupted their daily routines and had brought a new vitality to every part of their existence. They had left their village, followed that stranger and his friends, and discovered a whole new reality hidden behind the veil of their ordinary activities — a reality in which forgiveness, healing, and love were no longer mere words but powers touching the very core of their humanity. The stranger from Nazareth had made everything new. He had made them into people for whom the world was no longer a burden but a challenge, no longer a field of snares but a place with endless opportunities. He had brought joy and peace to their daily experience. He had made their life into a dance!

Now he is dead. His body that had radiated light had been destroyed under the hands of his torturers. His limbs had been ploughed by the instruments of violence and hatred, his eyes had become empty holes, his hands had lost their grip, his feet their firmness. He had become a nobody among nobodies. All had come to nothing. They had lost him. Not just him, but, with him, also themselves. The energy that had filled their days and nights had left them completely. They had become two lost human beings, walking home without having a home, returning to what had become a dark memory.

In many ways we are like them. We know it when we dare to look into the center of our being and encounter there our lostness. Aren't we lost too?

If there is any word that summarizes well our pain, it is the word "loss." We have lost so much! Sometimes it even seems that life is just one long series of losses. When we were born we lost the safety of the womb, when we went to school we lost the security of our family life, when we got our first job we lost the freedom of youth, when we got married or ordained we lost the joy of many options, and when we grew old we lost our good looks, our old friends, or our fame. When we became weak or ill, we lost our physical independence, and when we die we will lose it all! And these losses are part of the ordinary life! But whose life is ordinary? The losses that settle themselves deeply in our hearts and minds are the loss of intimacy through separations, the loss of safety through violence, the loss of innocence through abuse, the loss of friends through betrayal, the loss of love through abandonment, the loss of home through war, the loss of well-being through hunger, heat, and cold, the loss of children through illness or accidents, the loss of country through political upheaval, and the loss of life through earthquakes, floods, plane crashes, bombings, and diseases.

Perhaps many of these dark losses are far away from most of us; maybe they belong to the world of newspapers and television screens, but nobody can escape the agonizing losses that are part of our everyday existence — the loss of our dreams. We had thought so long of ourselves as successful, liked, and deeply loved. We had hoped for a life of generosity, service, and self-sacrifice. We had planned to become forgiving, caring, and always gentle people. We had a vision of ourselves

as reconcilers and peacemakers. But somehow –
we aren't even sure of what happened – we lost
our dream. We became worrying, anxious people
clinging to the few things we had collected and ex-
changing with one another news of the political,
social, and ecclesiastical scandals of the day. It is
this loss of spirit that is often hardest to acknowl-
edge and most difficult to confess.

But beyond all of these things there is the loss
of faith – the loss of the conviction that our life
has meaning. For a time we were able to bear our
losses and even to live them with fortitude and
perseverance because we lived them as losses that
would bring us closer to God. The pain and suffering of life were bearable because we lived them
as ways to test our will power and deepen our
conviction. But as we grow older we discover that
what supported us for so many years – prayer,
worship, sacraments, community life, and a clear
knowledge of God's guiding love – has lost its grip
on us. Long-cherished ideas, long-practiced disci-
plines, and long-held customs of celebrating life
can no longer warm our hearts, and we no longer
understand why and how we were so motivated.
We remember the time that Jesus was so real for us
that we had no question about his presence in our
lives. He was our most intimate friend, our coun-
selor and guide. He gave us comfort, courage, and
confidence. We could feel him, yes, taste and touch

him. And now? We no longer think of him very much, we no longer desire to spend long hours in his presence. We no longer have that special feeling about him. We even wonder if he is more than just a figure out of a story book. Many of our friends laugh at him, mock his name, or simply ignore him. Gradually we have come to the realization that for us too he has become a stranger — somehow we lost him.

I am not trying to suggest that all of these losses will touch each of our lives. But as we walk together and listen to each other we will soon discover that many, if not most, of these losses are part of the journey, our own journey or the journey of our companions.

What to do with our losses? That's the first question that faces us. Are we hiding them? Are we going to live as if they weren't real? Are we going to keep them away from our fellow travelers? Are we going to convince ourselves or others that our losses are little compared to our gains? Are we going to blame someone? We do all of these things most of the time, but there is another possibility: the possibility of mourning. Yes, we must mourn our losses. We cannot talk or act them away, but we can shed tears over them and allow ourselves to grieve deeply. To grieve is to allow our losses to tear apart feelings of security and safety and lead us to the painful truth of our brokenness. Our grief makes us experience the abyss of our own life in which nothing is settled, clear, or obvious, but everything constantly shifting and changing.

And as we feel the pain of our own losses, our grieving hearts open our inner eye to a world in which losses are suffered far beyond our own little world of family, friends, and colleagues. It is the world of prisoners, refugees, AIDS patients, starving children, and the countless human beings living in constant fear. Then the pain of our crying hearts connects us with the moaning and groaning of a suffering humanity. Then our mourning becomes larger than ourselves.

But in the midst of all this pain, there is a strange, shocking, yet very surprising voice. It is the voice of the one who says: "Blessed are those who mourn: they shall be comforted." That's the unexpected news: there is a blessing hidden in our grief. Not those who comfort are blessed, but those who mourn! Somehow, in the midst of our tears, a gift is hidden. Somehow, in the midst of our mourning, the first steps of the dance take place. Somehow, the cries that well up from our losses belong to our songs of gratitude.

We come to the Eucharist with hearts broken by many losses, our own as well as those of the world. Like the two disciples who walked home to their village we say: "Our hope had been ... but we lost hope. Torture and death have come instead." Our heads are no longer erect, looking forward, but "downcast" and bent to the ground.

This is how the journey starts. The question is whether our losses lead to resentment or to gratitude. Resentment is a real option. Many choose it. When we are hit by one loss after another, it is very easy to become disillusioned, angry, bitter, and increasingly resentful. The older we become, the greater is the temptation to say: "Life has cheated me. There is no future for me, nothing to hope for. The only thing to do is to defend the little I have left, so that I won't lose it all."

Resentment is one of the most destructive forces in our lives. It is cold anger that has settled into the center of our being and hardened our hearts. Resentment can become a way of life that so pervades our words and actions that we no longer recognize it as such.

I often wonder how I would live if there were no resentment at all in my heart. I am so used to talking about people I do not like, to harboring memories about events that gave me much pain, or to acting with suspicion and fear that I do not know how it would be if there were nothing to complain about and nobody to gripe about! My heart still has many corners that hide my resentments and I wonder if I really want to be without them. What would I do without these resentments? And there are many moments in life in which I have the opportunity to nurture them. Before breakfast I have already had many feelings of suspicion, jealousy, many thoughts about people I prefer to avoid, and many little plans to live my day in a guarded way. I wonder if there are any people without resentments. Resentment is such an obvious response to our many losses. The tragedy is that much resentment is hidden within the church. It is one of the most paralyzing aspects of the Christian community.

Still, the Eucharist presents another option. It is the possibility to choose, not resentment, but gratitude. Mourning our losses is the first step away from resentment and toward gratitude. The tears of our grief can soften our hardened hearts and open us to the possibility to say "thanks."

The word "Eucharist" means literally "act of thanksgiving." To celebrate the Eucharist and to live a Eucharistic life has everything to do with gratitude. Living Eucharistically is living life as a gift, a gift for which one is grateful. But gratitude is not the most obvious response to life, certainly not when we experience life as a series of losses! Still, the great mystery we celebrate in the Eucharist and live in a Eucharistic life is precisely that through mourning our losses we come to know life as a gift. The beauty and preciousness of life is intimately linked with its fragility and mortality. We can experience that every day — when we take a flower in our hands, when we see a butterfly dance in the air, when we caress a little baby. Fragility and giftedness are both there, and our joy is connected with both.

Each Eucharist begins with a cry for God's mercy. There is probably no prayer in the history of Christianity that has been prayed so frequently and intimately as the prayer "Lord, have mercy." It is the prayer that not only stands at the beginning of all Eucharistic liturgies of the West but also sounds as an ongoing cry through all Eastern liturgies. Lord, have mercy, *Kyrie Eleison, Gospody Pomiloe.* It's the cry of God's people, the cry of people with a contrite heart.

This cry for mercy is possible only when we are willing to confess that somehow, somewhere, we ourselves have something to do with our losses. Crying for mercy is a recognition that blaming God, the world, or others for our losses does not do full justice to the truth of who we are. At the moment we are willing to take responsibility, even for the pain we didn't cause directly; blaming is converted into an acknowledgment of our own role in human brokenness. The prayer for God's mercy comes from a heart that knows that this human brokenness is not a fatal condition of which we have become the sad victims, but the bitter fruit of the human choice to say "No" to love. The disciples who walked home to Emmaus were sad because they had lost the one in whom they had put all their hope, but they were also deeply aware that their own leaders had crucified him. Somehow they knew that their grief was connected with evil, an evil that they could recognize in their own hearts.

Celebrating the Eucharist requires that we stand in this world accepting our co-responsibility for the evil that surrounds and pervades us. As long as we remain stuck in our complaints about the terrible times in which we live and the terrible situations we have to bear and the terrible fate we have to suffer, we can never come to contrition. And contrition can grow only out of a contrite heart. When our losses are pure fate, our gains are pure luck! Fate does not lead to contrition, nor luck to gratitude.

Indeed, the conflicts in our personal lives as well as the conflicts on regional, national, or world scales are *our* conflicts, and only by claiming responsibility for them can we move beyond them — choosing a life of forgiveness, peace, and love.

The *Kyrie Eleison* — Lord, have mercy — must emerge from a contrite heart. In contrast to a hardened heart, a contrite heart is a heart that does not blame but acknowledges its own part in the sinfulness of the world and so has been made ready to receive God's mercy.

I still remember an evening meditation on Dutch

television during which the speaker poured water on hard, dried-out soil, saying, "Look, the soil cannot receive the water and no seed can grow." Then, after crumbling the soil with his hands and pouring water on it again, he said, "It is only the broken soil that can receive the water and make the seed grow and bear fruit."

After seeing this I understood what it meant to begin the Eucharist with a contrite heart, a heart broken open, to receive the water of God's grace.

But how is it possible to begin a thanksgiving celebration with a broken heart? Don't the acknowledgment of our sinful condition and the awareness of our co-responsibility for the evil in the world paralyze us? Isn't a true confession of sins too debilitating? Yes, it is! But no sin can be faced without some knowledge of grace. No loss can be mourned without some intuition that we will find new life.

When the disciples walking to Emmaus told their story about their great loss, they also told that strange story about the women who had found the tomb empty and had seen angels. But they were sceptical and doubtful. Wasn't he crucified a few days ago? Hadn't everything come to an end? Hadn't evil finally won? So what about these women's tales that he was alive? Who could take that seriously? But then again, they had to say, "Some of our friends went to the tomb and found everything exactly as the women had reported, but of him they saw nothing!"

That's how we generally approach the Eucharist. With a strange mixture of despair and hope. Part of us looking at our own life and the lives of those around us wants to say, "Let's forget about it. It's all over. Oh, sure we thought about a better world, imagined a new community of love, and dreamt about a time in which all people would live together in peace. But the truth has caught up with us. We now know that all of this was little more than an illusion. Our unchangeable character and persistent bad habits, our jealousies and resentments, our moments of anger and revenge, our uncontrollable violence, the countless signs of human cruelty, the crimes, the torture, the wars, the exploitations – all of these have surely woken us up to the bitter truth that our youthful hope has been crucified."

And still – the other stories remain and continue to appear. Stories about a few people who saw it differently, stories about gestures of forgiveness and healing, stories about goodness, beauty, and truth. And as we listen carefully to the deeper voices in our heart we realize that beneath our scepticism and cynicism there is a yearning for love, unity, and communion that doesn't go away even when there remain so many arguments to dismiss it as sentimental childhood memories.

"Lord, Have Mercy"

"Lord, have mercy, Lord, have mercy, Lord, have mercy." That's the prayer that keeps emerging from the depth of our being and breaking through the walls of our cynicism. Yes, we are sinners, hopeless sinners; everything is lost and nothing is left of our hopes and dreams. Still, there is a voice: "My grace is enough for you!" and we cry again for the healing of our cynical hearts and dare to believe that, indeed, in the midst of our mourning, we can find a gift to be grateful for. But for this discovery we need a special companion!

II

Discerning
the Presence

"This Is the Word of God"

As the two travelers walk home mourning their loss, Jesus comes up and walks by their side, but their eyes are prevented from recognizing him. Suddenly there are no longer two but three people walking, and everything becomes different. The two friends no longer look down at the ground in front of them but into the eyes of the stranger who has joined them and asked, "What are all these things you are discussing as you walk along?" There is some astonishment, even agitation: "You must be the only person who does not know the things that have been happening!" Then there follows a long story: the story of loss, the story of puzzling news about an empty tomb. Here at least is someone to listen, someone who is willing to hear the words of disillusionment, sadness, and utter confusion. Nothing seems to make sense. But it is better to tell a stranger than to repeat the known facts to each other.

Then something happens! Something shifts. The stranger begins to speak, and his words ask for serious attention. He had listened to them; now they listened to him. His words are very clear and straightforward. He speaks of things they already knew: their long past with all that had happened during the centuries before they were born, the story of Moses who led their people to freedom, and the story of the prophets who challenged their people never to let go of their dearly acquired freedom. It was an all-too-familiar story. Still it sounded as if they were hearing it for the first time.

The difference lay in the storyteller! A stranger appearing from nowhere yet one who, somehow, seems closer than anyone who had ever told that story. The loss, the grief, the guilt, the fear, the glimpses of hope, and the many unanswered questions that battled for attention in their restless minds, all of these were lifted up by this stranger and placed in the context of a story much larger than their own. What had seemed so confusing began to offer new horizons; what had seemed so oppressive began to feel liberating; what had seemed so extremely sad began to take on the quality of joy! As he talked to them, they gradually came to know that their little lives weren't as little as they had thought, but part of a great mystery that not only embraced many generations, but stretched itself out from eternity to eternity.

The stranger didn't say that there was no reason for sadness, but that their sadness was part of a larger sadness in which joy was hidden. The stranger didn't say that the death they were mourning wasn't real, but that it was a death that inaugurated even more life – real life. The stranger didn't say that they hadn't lost a friend who had given them new courage and new hope, but that this loss would create the way to a relationship far beyond any friendship they had ever experienced. Never did the stranger deny what they told him. To the contrary, he affirmed it as part of a much larger event in which they were allowed to play a unique role.

Still, this was not a soothing conversation. The stranger was strong, direct, unsentimental. There were no easy consolations. It even seemed that he pierced their complaints with a truth they might have preferred not to know. After all, continual complaining is more attractive than facing reality. But the stranger was not the least bit afraid to break through their defenses and to call them far beyond their own narrowness of mind and heart.

"Foolish people," he said. "So slow to believe." These words go straight to the hearts of the two men. "Foolish" is a hard word, a word that offends us and makes us defensive. But it can also crack open a cover of fear and self-consciousness and lead to a whole new knowledge of being human. It is a wake-up call, a ripping off of blindfolds, a tearing down of useless protective devices. You foolish

41

people, don't you see – don't you hear – don't you know? You have been looking at a little bush not realizing that you are on the top of a mountain that offers you a worldwide view. You have been staring at an obstacle not willing to consider that the obstacle was put there to show you the right path. You have been complaining about your losses, not realizing that these losses are there to enable you to receive the gift of life.

The stranger had to call them "foolish" to make them see. And what is the challenge? To trust. They didn't trust that their experience was more than the experience of an irretrievable loss. They didn't trust that there was anything else to do than to go home and take up their old way of living again. "Foolish people . . . so slow to believe." Slow to believe; slow to trust in the larger scheme of things; slow to jump over their many complaints and discover the wide spectrum of new opportunities; slow to move beyond the pains of the moment and see them as part of a much larger healing process.

This slowness is not an innocent slowness because it can entrap us in our complaints and narrowmindedness. It is the slowness that can prevent us from discovering the landscape in which we live. It is quite possible to come to the end of our lives without ever having known who we are and what we are meant to become. Life is short. We cannot simply expect that the little we see, hear, and experience will reveal to us the whole of our existence. We are too near-sighted and too hard of hearing for that. Someone has to open our eyes and ears and help us to discover what lies beyond our own perception. Someone has to make our hearts burn!

Jesus joins us as we walk in sadness and explains the scriptures to us. But we do not know that it is Jesus. We think of him as a stranger who knows less than we do of what is happening in our lives. And still – we know something, we sense something, we intuit something: our hearts begin to burn. At the very moment that he is with us we can't fully understand what is happening. We can't speak about it to each other. Later, yes later, when it is all over, we might be able to say, "Did not our hearts burn within us as he talked to us on the road and explained the scriptures to us?" But when he walks with us it is all too close for reflection.

It is with this mysterious presence that the "service of the Word" during each Eucharist wants to bring us in touch, and it is this same mysterious presence that is constantly revealed to us as we live our lives Eucharistically. The readings from the Old and New Testaments and the homily that follows these readings are given to us to discern his presence as he walks with us in our sadness. Each day there are different readings; each day there is a different word of explanation or exhortation. Each day there are words to accompany us. We cannot live without words that come from God, words to pull us out of our sadness and lift us up to a place from where we can discover what we are truly living.

It is important to know that, although these words, read or spoken, are there to inform, instruct, or inspire us, their first significance is that they make Jesus himself present to us. On our journey, Jesus explains to us the passages that are about himself. Whether we read the book of Exodus, the Psalms, the Prophets, or the Gospels, they are all there to make our hearts burn. The Eucharistic presence is first of all a presence through the word. Without that presence through the word, we won't be able to recognize his presence in the breaking of the bread.

We live in a world where words are cheap. Words engulf us. In advertisements, on billboards and traffic signs, in pamphlets, booklets, and books, on blackboards, overhead projectors, flip-charts, screens, and newsrunners. Words move, flicker, turn around, grow bigger, brighter, and fatter. They are presented to us in all sizes and colors — but finally we say, "Well, they are just words." Increased in number, words have decreased in value. Their main value seems to be informational. Words inform us. We need words in order to know what to do or how to do it, where to go and how to get there.

It is not surprising, then, that the words in the Eucharist are listened to mostly as words that inform us. They tell us a story, they instruct, they admonish. Since most of us have heard these words before, they seldom touch us deeply. Often we scarcely pay attention to them; they have become too familiar. We don't expect to be surprised or touched. We listen to them as to "the same old story" – whether read from a book or spoken from a pulpit.

The tragedy is that the word then loses its sacramental quality. The Word of God is sacramental. That means it is sacred, and as a sacred word it makes present what it indicates. When Jesus spoke to the two sad travelers on the road and explained to them the words of scriptures that were about himself, their hearts began to burn, that is to say, they experienced his presence. Speaking about himself he became present to them. With his words he did much more than simply make them think of him, or instruct them about himself, or inspire them with his memory. Through his words he became really present to them. This is what we mean by the sacramental quality of the word. The word creates what it expresses. The Word of God is always sacramental. In the book of Genesis we are told that God created the world, but in Hebrew the words for "speaking" and for "creating" are the same word. Literally translated it says, "God spoke light and light was." For God, speaking is creating. When we say that God's word is sacred, we mean that God's word is full of God's presence. On the road to Emmaus, Jesus became present through his word, and it was that presence that transformed sadness to joy and mourning to dancing. This is what happens in every Eucharist. The word that is read and spoken wants to lead us into God's presence and transform our hearts and minds. Often we think about the word as an exhortation to go out and change our lives. But the full power of the word lies, not in how we apply it to our lives after we have heard it, but in its transforming power that does its divine work as we listen.

The Gospels are filled with examples of God's presence in the word. Personally, I am always touched by the story of Jesus in the synagogue of Nazareth. There he read from Isaiah:

The Spirit of the Lord is on me,
for he has anointed me
to bring good news to the afflicted.
He has sent me to proclaim liberty to captives,
sight to the blind,
to let the oppressed go free,
to proclaim a year of favor from the Lord.
(Luke 4:18–19)

After having read these words, Jesus said, "This text is being fulfilled today even while you are listening." Suddenly, it becomes clear that the afflicted, the captives, the blind, and the oppressed are not people somewhere outside of the synagogue who, someday, will be liberated; they are the people who are listening. And it is in the listening that God becomes present and heals.

The Word of God is not a word to apply in our daily lives at some later date; it is a word to heal us through, and in, our listening here and now.

The questions therefore are: How does God come to me as I listen to the word? Where do I discern the healing hand of God touching me through the word? How are my sadness, my grief, and my mourning being transformed at this very moment? Do I sense the fire of God's love purifying my heart and giving me new life? These questions lead me to the sacrament of the word, the sacred place of God's real presence.

At first this might sound quite new for a person living in a society in which the main value of the word is its applicability. But most of us know already, generally unconsciously, of the healing and destroying power of the spoken word. When someone says to me, "I love you," or "I hate you," I am not just receiving some useful information. These words *do* something in me. They make my blood move, my heart beat, my breathing speed up. They make me feel and think differently. They lift me up to a new way of being and give me another knowledge of myself. These words have the power to heal or to destroy me.

When Jesus joins us on the road and explains the scriptures to us, we must listen with our whole being, trusting that the word that created us will also heal us. God wants to become present to us and thus radically transform our fearful hearts.

The sacramental quality of the word makes God present not only as an intimate personal presence, but also as a presence that gives us a place in the great story of salvation. The God who becomes present to us is not only the God of our heart, but also the God of Abraham and Sarah, Isaac and Rebecca, Jacob and Leah, the God of Isaiah and Jeremiah, the God of David and Solomon, the God of Peter and Paul, of St. Francis and Dorothy Day — the God whose world-embracing love is revealed to us in Jesus, the companion on our journey.

The word of the Eucharist makes us part of the great story of our salvation. Our little stories are lifted up into God's great story and there given their unique place. The word lifts us up and makes us see that our daily, ordinary lives are, in fact, sacred lives that play a necessary role in the fulfillment of God's promises. The written and spoken word of the Eucharist allow us to say with Mary, "He has looked upon the humiliation of his servant. Yes, from now on all generations will call me blessed, for the Almighty has done great things for me ... mindful of his mercy to Abraham and to his descendants forever."

Here we see that the Eucharist, as we celebrate it in the sacred liturgy, calls us to a Eucharistic life, a life in which we are continuously aware of our role in the sacred story of God's redemptive presence through all generations. The great temptation of our lives is to deny our role as chosen people and so allow ourselves to be trapped in the worries of our daily lives. Without the word that keeps lifting us up as God's chosen people, we remain, or become, small people, stuck in the complaints that emerge from our daily struggle to survive. Without the word that makes our hearts burn, we can't do much more than walk home, resigned to the sad fact that there is nothing new under the sun. Without the word, our life has little meaning, little vitality, and little energy. Without the word we remain little people with little concerns who live little lives and die little deaths. Without the word we still may be a news item in the local or even a national newspaper for a day or two, but there will be no generations to call us blessed. Without the word our isolated pains and sorrows may extinguish the Spirit within and make us victims of bitterness and resentment.

We need the word spoken and explained by the

one who joins us on the road and makes his presence known to us – a presence first discerned in our burning hearts. It is this presence that encourages us to let go of our hardened hearts and become grateful. As grateful people we can invite into the intimacy of our home the one who has made our hearts burn.

III

Inviting
the Stranger

"I Believe"

s they listen to the stranger, something changes within the two sad travelers. Not only do they sense a new hope and a new joy touching their innermost being, but their walk has become less hesitant. The stranger has given them a new sense of direction. "Going home" no longer means returning to the only place left to go. Home has become more than a necessary shelter, a house where they can stay as long as they don't know what else to do. The stranger has given their journey a new meaning. Their empty house has become a place of welcome, a place to receive guests, a place to continue the conversation they had so unexpectedly begun.

When you are feeling only your losses, then everything around you speaks of them. The trees, the flowers, the clouds, the hills and valleys, they all reflect your sadness. They all become mourners. When your dearest friend has died, all of nature speaks of her. The wind whispers her name, the branches, heavy with leaves, weep for her, and the dahlias and rhododendrons offer their petals to cover her body. But as you keep walking forward with someone at your side, opening your heart to the mysterious truth that your friend's death was not just the end but also a new beginning, not just the cruelty of fate, but the necessary way to freedom, not just an ugly and gruesome destruction, but a suffering leading to glory, then you can gradually discern a new song sounding through creation, and going home corresponds to the deepest desire of your heart.

Of all the words the stranger had spoken, there was one that stands out in the travelers' mind: "Glory." "Was it not necessary," he had said, "that the Christ should suffer before entering into his glory?" Their hearts and minds were still so full of the images of death and destruction. And now here was that word "Glory." It didn't seem to fit, and still, spoken by this stranger, it sets their hearts on fire and makes them see what they had not been able to see before. It was as if they had seen only the manure that covered the soil, but never the fruits on the trees that had sprung from it. Glory, light, splendor, beauty, truth — they all seemed so unreal and unreachable! But now there were new sounds in the air and new colors in the fields. Going home had become a good thing. Home calls us. Home is where the table is — the table to sit around, to eat and drink with friends!

And the stranger? Hasn't he become a friend? He makes our hearts burn, he opens our eyes and ears. He is our companion on the journey! Home has become a good place for the friend to come. So they say, "It's nearly evening, and the day is almost over . . . come and stay with us." He doesn't ask for an invitation. He doesn't beg for a place to stay. In fact, he acts as if he wants to go on. But they insist that he come in; they even press him to stay with them. He accepts. He goes in to stay with them.

Maybe we are not used to thinking about the Eucharist as an invitation to Jesus to stay with us. We are more inclined to think about Jesus inviting us to his house, his table, his meal. But Jesus wants to be invited. Without an invitation he will go on to other places. It is very important to realize that Jesus never forces himself on us. Unless we invite him, he will always remain a stranger, possibly a very attractive, intelligent stranger with whom we had an interesting conversation, but a stranger nevertheless.

Even after he has taken much of our sadness away and shown us that our lives are not as petty and small as we had assumed, he can still remain the one we met on the road, the remarkable person who crossed our path and spoke with us for a while, the unusual personality about whom we can speak to our family and friends.

I have many memories of encounters with people who made my heart burn but whom I did not invite into my home. Sometimes it happens on a long plane trip, sometimes in a train, sometimes at a party. Afterwards I say to my friends: "Let me tell you whom I met today. A quite fascinating person. He said things so remarkable that I couldn't believe what I heard. It seemed that he knew me intimately. Yes, he could read my thoughts and speak to me as if he had known me for a long time. Quite special, quite unique, astonishing even. I wish you could have met him! But he went on to... I don't know where!"

Interesting, stimulating, and inspiring as all these strangers may be, when I do not invite them into my home, nothing truly happens. I might have a few new ideas, but my life remains basically the same. Without an invitation, which is the expression of the desire for a lasting relationship, the good news that we have heard cannot bear lasting fruit. It remains "news" among the many types of news that bombard us every day.

It is one of the characteristics of our contemporary society that encounters, good as they may be, don't become deep relationships. Thus our life is filled with good advice, helpful ideas, wonderful perspectives, but they are simply added to the many other ideas and perspectives and so leave us "uncommitted." In a society with such an informational overload, even the most significant encounters can be reduced to "something interesting" among many other interesting things.

Only with an invitation to "come and stay with me" can an interesting encounter develop into a transforming relationship.

One of the most decisive moments of the Eucharist — and of our life — is the moment of invitation. Do we say: "It was wonderful to meet you, thank you for your insights, your advice, and your encouragement. I hope the rest of your journey goes well. Goodbye!" Or do we say: "I have heard you, my heart is changing ... please come into my home and see where and how I live!" This invitation to come and see is the invitation that makes all the difference.

Jesus is a very interesting person; his words are full of wisdom. His presence is heart-warming. His gentleness and kindness are deeply moving. His message is very challenging. But do we invite him into our home? Do we want him to come to know us behind the walls of our most intimate life? Do we want to introduce him to all the people we live with? Do we want him to see us in our everyday lives? Do we want him to touch us where we are most vulnerable? Do we want him to enter into the back rooms of our homes, rooms that we ourselves prefer to keep safely locked? Do we truly want him to stay with us when it is nearly evening and the day is almost over?

The Eucharist requires this invitation. Having listened to his word, we have to be able to say more than, "This is interesting!" We have to dare to say, "I trust you; I entrust myself, with all my being, body, mind, and soul to you. I don't want to keep any secrets from you. You can see everything I do and hear everything I say. I don't want you to be a stranger any longer. I want you to become my most intimate friend. I want you to know me, not only as I walk on the road and talk to my fellow travelers, but also as I find myself alone with my innermost feelings and thoughts. And most of all, I want to come to know you, not just as my companion on the journey, but as the companion of my soul."

Saying this is not easy, since we are fearful people, and we do not easily entrust every part of ourselves to others. Our fear of being completely open and vulnerable is equal to our desire to know and to be known.

I even hide parts of myself from myself! There are thoughts, feelings, and emotions that are so disturbing to me that I prefer to live as if they were not there.

If I do not trust myself how can I trust anyone else? Still my deepest desire is to love and to be loved, and that is possible only if I am willing to know and to be known.

Jesus reveals himself to us as the Good Shepherd

who knows us intimately and loves us. But do we
want to be known by him? Do we want him to walk
freely into every room of our inner lives? Do we
want him to see our bad side as well as our good,
our shadow as well as our light? Or do we prefer
him to go on without entering our home? In the
end, the question is: "Do we really trust him and
entrust every part of ourselves to him?"

When, after the readings and the homily, we say:
"I believe in God, Father, Son, and Holy Spirit, in
the Catholic Church, the communion of saints, the
forgiveness of sins, the resurrection of the body,
and life everlasting," we invite Jesus into our home
and entrust ourselves to his Way.

As a moment of the Eucharistic celebration and,
even more, of our Eucharistic life, the Creed is
much more than a summary of the doctrine of the
church. It is a profession of faith. And "faith," as
the Greek word *pistis* shows, is an act of trust. It
is the great "Yes." It says "Yes" to the one who has
explained the scriptures to us as scriptures that are
about him. It is this deep "Yes," not only to the
words he spoke but also to him who spoke them,
that brings us finally to the table. If we can say,
"Yes, we trust you and entrust our lives to you," we
go beyond just walking into his presence; we dare
to open ourselves to communion with him.

The two traveling friends invite, indeed, press,
the stranger to stay with them. "Be our guest," they

say. They want to be his hosts. They invite the stranger to lay aside his strangeness and become a friend to them. That's what true hospitality is all about, to offer a safe place, where the stranger can become friend. There were two friends and a stranger. But now there are three friends, sharing the same table.

The table is the place of intimacy. Around the table we discover each other. It's the place where we pray. It's the place where we ask: "How was your day?" It's the place where we eat and drink together and say: "Come on, take some more!" It is the place of old and new stories. It is the place for smiles and tears. The table, too, is the place where distance is most painfully felt. It is the place where the children feel the tension between the parents, where brothers and sisters express their anger and jealousies, where accusations are made, and where plates and cups become instruments of violence. Around the table, we know whether there is friendship and community or hatred and division. Precisely because the table is the place of intimacy for all the members of the household, it is also the place where the absence of that intimacy is most painfully revealed.

When, on the evening before his death, Jesus came together with his disciples around the table, he revealed both intimacy and distance. He shared the bread and the cup as a sign of friendship, but he also said, "Look, here with me on the table is the hand of the man who is betraying me."

When I think about my own youth, I think most often of our family meals, especially on feast days. I remember the Christmas decorations, the birthday cakes, the Easter candles, and the smiling faces. But I also remember the words of anger, the walking away, the tears, the embarrassment, and the seemingly endless silences.

We are most vulnerable when we sleep or eat together. Bed and table are the two places of intimacy. Also the two places of greatest pain. And, maybe, of these two places, the table is the most important because it is the place where all who belong to the household gather and where family, community, friendship, hospitality, and true generosity can be expressed and made real.

Jesus accepts the invitation to come into the home of his traveling companions, and he sits down at table with them. They offer him the place of honor. He is in the center. They are alongside him. They look at him. He looks at them. There is intimacy, friendship, community. Then something new happens. Something scarcely noticeable to an untrained eye. Jesus is the guest of his disciples, but as soon as he enters into their home, he becomes their host! And as their host he invites them to enter into full communion with him.

IV

Entering
into Communion

"Take and Eat"

hen Jesus enters into the home of his disciples, it becomes his home. The guest becomes host. He who was invited now invites. The two disciples who trusted the stranger enough to let him enter into their inner space are now led into the inner life of their host. "Now while he was with them at table, he took the bread and said the blessing; then he broke it and handed it to them." So simple, so ordinary, so obvious, and still — so very different! What else can you do when you share bread with your friends? You take it, bless it, break it, and give it. That is what bread is for: to be taken, blessed, broken, and given. Nothing new, nothing surprising. It happens every day, in countless homes. It belongs to the essence of living. We can't really live without bread that is taken, blessed, broken, and given. Without it there is no table fellowship, no community, no bond of friendship, no peace, no love, no hope. Yet, with it, all can become new!

Maybe we have forgotten that the Eucharist is a simple human gesture. The vestments, the candles, the altar servers, the large books, the outstretched arms, the large altar, the songs, the people — nothing seems very simple, very ordinary, very obvious. We often need a booklet to follow the ceremony and understand its meaning. Still, nothing is meant to be different from what happened in that little village among the three friends. There is bread on the table; there is wine on the table. The bread is taken, blessed, broken, and given. The wine is taken, blessed, and given. That is what happens around each table that wants to be a table of peace.

Every time we invite Jesus into our homes, that is to say, into our life with all its light and dark sides, and offer him the place of honor at our table, he takes the bread and the cup and hands them to us saying: "Take and eat, this is my body. Take and drink, this is my blood. Do this to remember me." Are we surprised? Not really! Wasn't our heart burning when he talked to us on the road? Didn't we already know that he was not a stranger to us? Weren't we already aware that the one who was crucified by our leaders was alive and with us? Hadn't we seen it before, that he took the bread, blessed it, broke it, and gave it to us? He did so before the large crowd who had listened for long hours to his word, he did it in the upper room before Judas handed him over to suffering, and he has done it countless times when we have come to the end of a long day and he joins us around the table for a simple meal.

The Eucharist is the most ordinary and the most divine gesture imaginable. That is the truth of Jesus. So human, yet so divine; so familiar, yet so mysterious; so close, yet so revealing! But that is the story of Jesus who "being in the form of God did not count equality with God something to be grasped, but emptied himself, taking the form of a slave, becoming as human beings are; and being in every way like a human being, he was humbler yet, even to accepting death, death on a cross" (Phil. 2:18). It is the story of God who wants to come close to us, so close that we can see him with our own eyes, hear him with our own ears, touch him with our own hands; so close that there is nothing between us and him, nothing that separates, nothing that divides, nothing that creates distance.

Jesus is God-for-us, God-with-us, God-within-us. Jesus is God giving himself completely, pouring himself out for us without reserve. Jesus doesn't hold back or cling to his own possessions. He gives all there is to give. "Eat, drink, this is my body, this is my blood . . . this is me for you!"

We all know of this desire to give ourselves at the table. We say: "Eat and drink; I made this for you. Take more; it is there for you to enjoy, to be strengthened, yes, to feel how much I love you." What we desire is not simply to give food, but to give ourselves. "Be my guest," we say. And as we encourage our friends to eat from our table, we want to say, "Be my friend, be my companion, be my love — be part of my life — I want to give myself to you."

In the Eucharist, Jesus gives all. The bread is not simply a sign of his desire to become our food; the cup is not just a sign of his willingness to be our drink. Bread and wine *become* his body and blood in the giving. The bread, indeed, is his body given for us; the wine his blood poured out for us. As God becomes fully present for us in Jesus, so Jesus becomes fully present to us in the bread and the wine of the Eucharist. God not only became flesh for us years ago in a country far away. God also becomes food and drink for us now at this moment of the Eucharistic celebration, right where we are together around the table. God does not hold back; God gives all. That is the mystery of the Incarnation. That too is the mystery of the Eucharist. Incarnation and Eucharist are the two expressions of the immense, self-giving love of God. And so the sacrifice on the cross and the sacrifice at the table are one sacrifice, one complete, divine self-giving that reaches out to all humanity in time and space.

The word that best expresses this mystery of God's total self-giving love is "communion." It is the word that contains the truth that, in and through Jesus, God wants, not only to teach us, instruct us, or inspire us, but to become one with us. God desires to be fully united with us so that all of God and all of us can be bound together in a lasting love. The whole long history of God's relationship with us human beings is a history of ever-deepening communion. It is not simply a history of unities, separations, and restored unities, but a history in which God searches for ever-new ways to commune intimately with those created in God's own image.

Augustine said: "My soul is restless until it rests in you, O God," but when I examine the tortuous story of our own salvation, I see not only that we are yearning to belong to God, but that God also is yearning to belong to us. It seems as if God is crying out to us: "My heart is restless until I may rest in you, my beloved creation." From Adam and Eve to Abraham and Sarah, from Abraham and Sarah to David and Bathsheba, and from David and Bathsheba to Jesus and ever since, God cries out to be received by his own. "I created you, I gave you all my love, I guided you, offered you my support, promised you the fulfillment of your hearts' desires: where are you, where is your response, where is your love? What else must I do to make you love me? I won't give up, I will keep trying. One day, you will discover how I long for your love!"

God desires communion: a unity that is vital and alive, an intimacy that comes from both sides, a bond that is truly mutual. Nothing forced or "willed," but a communion freely offered and received. God goes all the way to make this communion possible. God becomes a child dependent on human care, a boy in need of guidance, a teacher searching for students, a prophet crying for followers, and, finally, a dead man pierced by a soldier's lance and laid in a tomb. At the very end of the story, he stands there looking at us, asking with eyes full of tender expectation: "Do you love me?" and again, "Do you love me?" and a third time, "Do you love me?"

It is this intense desire of God to enter into the most intimate relationship with us that forms the core of the Eucharistic celebration and the Eucharistic life. God not only wants to enter human history by becoming a person who lives in a specific epoch and a specific country, but God wants to become our daily food and drink at any time and any place.

Therefore Jesus takes bread, blesses it, breaks it, and gives it to us. And then, as we see the bread in our hands and bring it to our mouths to eat it, yes, then our eyes are opened and we recognize him.

Eucharist is recognition. It is the full realization that the one who takes, blesses, breaks, and gives is the One who, from the beginning of time, has desired to enter into communion with us. Communion is what God wants and what we want. It is the deepest cry of God's and our heart, because we are made with a heart that can be satisfied only by the one who made it. God created in our heart a yearning for communion that no one but God can, and wants, to fulfill. God knows this. We seldom do. We keep looking somewhere else for that experience of belonging. We look at the splendor of nature, the excitement of history, and the attractiveness of people, but that simple breaking of the bread, so ordinary and unspectacular, seems such an unlikely place to find the communion for which we yearn. Still, if we have mourned our losses, listened to him on the road, and invited him into our innermost being, we will know that the communion we have been waiting to receive is the same communion he has been waiting to give.

There is one sentence in the Emmaus story that leads us right into the mystery of communion. It is the sentence: " ... they recognized him; but he had vanished from their sight." In the same moment that the two friends recognize him in the breaking of the bread, he is no longer there with them. When the bread is given them to eat, they no longer see him sitting with them at the table. When they eat, he has become invisible. When they enter into the most intimate communion with Jesus, the stranger — become friend — is no longer with them. Precisely when he becomes most present to them, he also becomes the absent one.

Here we touch one of the most sacred aspects of the Eucharist: the mystery that the deepest communion with Jesus is a communion that happens in his absence. The two disciples who walked on the road to Emmaus had listened to him for many hours, walked with him from village to village, helped him in his preaching, rested and taken meals with him. During the year, he had become their teacher, their guide, their master. All of their hopes for a new and better future were focused on him. Still ... they had never fully come to know him, to fully understand him. Often had he said to them: "Now you don't understand, but later you will." They didn't really know what he was trying to say. They thought they were closer to him than to any other person they had ever met. Still he kept saying: "I tell you this now ... so that later, when I am no longer with you, you will remember and understand." One day he had even said that it was good for him to go so that his Spirit could come and lead them to full intimacy with him. His Spirit would open their eyes and make them fully understand who he is and why he had come to be with them.

All during his time with the disciples there had been no full communion. Yes, they had stayed with him and sat at his feet; yes, they had been his disciples, even his friends. But they had not yet entered into full communion with him. His body and blood and their body and blood had not yet become one. In many ways, he still had been the other, the one over there, the one who goes ahead of them and shows them the way. But when they eat the bread he gives them and they recognize him, that recognition is a deep spiritual awareness that, now, he dwells in their innermost being, that, now, he breathes in them, speaks in them, yes, lives in them. When they eat the bread that he hands them, their lives are transformed into his life. It is no longer they who live, but Jesus, the Christ, who lives in them. And right at that most sacred moment of communion, he has vanished from their sight.

This is what we live in the Eucharistic celebration. This too is what we live when we live a Eucharistic life. It is a communion so intimate, so holy, so sacred, and so spiritual that our corporeal senses can no longer reach it. No longer can we see him with our mortal eyes, hear him with our mortal ears, or touch him with our mortal bodies. He has come to us at that place within us where the powers of darkness and evil cannot reach, where death has no access.

When he reaches out to us and puts the bread in our hands and brings the cup to our lips, Jesus asks us to let go of the easier friendship we have had with him so far and to let go of the feelings, emotions, and even thoughts that belong to that friendship. When we eat of his body and drink of his blood, we accept the loneliness of not having him any longer at our table as a consoling partner in our conversation, helping us to deal with the losses of our daily life. It is the loneliness of the spiritual life, the loneliness of knowing that he is closer to us than we ever can be to ourselves. It's the loneliness of faith.

We will keep crying out, "Lord, have mercy"; we will keep listening to the scriptures and their meaning; we will keep saying, "Yes, I believe." But communion with him goes far beyond all of that. It brings us to the place where the light blinds our eyes and where our whole being is wrapped in not-seeing. It is at that place of communion that we cry out: "God, my God, why have you abandoned me?" It is at that place, too, that our emptiness gives us the prayer: "Father, into your hands I commend my Spirit."

Communion with Jesus means becoming like him. With him we are nailed on the cross, with him we are laid in the tomb, with him we are raised up to accompany lost travelers on their journey. Communion, becoming Christ, leads us to a new realm of being. It ushers us into the Kingdom. There the old distinctions between happiness and sadness, success and failure, praise and blame, health and sickness, life and death, no longer exist. There we no longer belong to the world that keeps dividing, judging, separating, and evaluating. There we belong to Christ and Christ to us, and with Christ we belong to God. Suddenly the two disciples, who ate the bread and recognized him, are alone again. But not with the aloneness with which they began their journey. They are alone, together, and know that a new bond has been created between them. They no longer look at the ground with downcast faces. They look at each other and say: "Did our hearts not burn when he talked to us on the road and explained the scriptures to us?"

Communion creates community. Christ, living in them, brought them together in a new way. The Spirit of the risen Christ, which entered them through the eating of the bread and drinking of the cup, not only made them recognize Christ himself but also each other as members of a new community of faith. Communion makes us look at each other and speak to each other, not about the latest news, but about him who walked with us. We discover each other as people who belong together because each of us now belongs to him. We are alone, because he disappeared from our sight, but we are together because each of us is in communion with him and so has become one body through him.

We ate his body, we drank his blood. In so doing, all of us who took from the same bread and the same cup have become one body. Communion creates community, because the God living in us makes us recognize the God in our fellow humans.

We cannot see God in the other person. Only God in us can see God in the other person. That is what we mean when we say, "Spirit speaks to Spirit, Heart speaks to Heart, God speaks to God." Our participation in the inner life of God leads us to a new way of participation in each other's lives.

This might sound very "unreal," but when we live it, it becomes more real than the "reality" of the world. As Paul says: "The blessing-cup, which we bless, is it not a sharing in the blood of Christ, and the loaf of bread which we break, is it not a sharing in the body of Christ? And as there is one loaf, so we, although there are many of us, are one single body, for we all share in the one loaf" (1 Cor. 16–17).

This new body is a spiritual body, fashioned by the Spirit of love. It manifests itself in very concrete ways: in forgiveness, reconciliation, mutual support, outreach to people in need, solidarity with all who suffer, and an ever-increasing concern for justice and peace. Thus communion not only creates community, but community always leads to mission.

V

Going
on a Mission

"Go and Tell"

Everything has changed. The losses are no longer felt as debilitating; home no longer is an empty place. The two travelers who started their journey with downcast faces now look at each other with eyes full of new light. The stranger, who had become friend, has given them his spirit, the divine spirit of joy, peace, courage, hope, and love. There is no doubt in their minds: He is alive! Not alive as before, not as the fascinating preacher and healer from Nazareth, but alive as a new breath within them. Cleopas and his friend have become new people. A new heart and a new spirit have been given to them. They also have become new friends for each other — no longer people who can offer each other consolation and support as they mourn their losses, but people with a new mission who, together, have something to say, something important, something urgent, something that cannot remain hidden, something that must be proclaimed. Happily they have each other.

Nobody would believe just one of them. But when they speak together they will get a fair hearing. The others need to know because they too had placed all their hope in him. There are the eleven who ate with him the evening before his death; there are the disciples, women and men, who had been with him for years. They need to know what has happened to them. They need to know that it is not all over. They need to know that he is alive and that they recognized him when he handed the bread to them. There is no time to waste. "Let's hurry," they say to each other. Quickly they put on their sandals, grab their coats and walking staffs, and are on their way back to their friends, back to those who still might not know that the women who had heard from the angels that he is alive are right. The story summarizes it all in a very few words: "They set out that instant and returned to Jerusalem."

What a difference between their "going home" and their return. It is the difference between doubt and faith, despair and hope, fear and love. It is the difference between two dispirited human beings dragging themselves along the road and two friends walking fast, running even at times, all excited about the news they have for their friends.

Returning to the city is not without danger. After the execution of Jesus, his disciples are afraid. They wonder what their fate will be. But having recognized their Lord, their fear is gone, and they are free to become witnesses of the resurrection — the costs notwithstanding. They realize that the same people who hated Jesus may hate them, that the same people who killed Jesus may kill them. Their return may indeed cost them their lives. They may be asked to witness, not only with words, but with their own blood. But they no longer fear martyrdom. The risen Lord, present in their innermost being, has filled them with a love stronger than death. Nothing can hold them back from returning home even when home no longer means a "safe" place.

The Eucharist concludes with a mission. "Go, now and tell!" The Latin words "Ite Missa est," with which the priest used to conclude the Mass, literally mean: "Go, this is your mission."

Communion is not the end. Mission is. Communion, that sacred intimacy with God, is not the final moment of the Eucharistic life. We recognized him, but that recognition is not just for us to savor or to keep as a secret. As Mary of Magdala, so too the two friends had heard deep in themselves the words "Go and tell." That's the conclusion of the Eucharistic celebration; that too is the final call of the Eucharistic life. "Go and tell. What you have heard and seen is not just for yourself. It is for the brothers and sisters and for all who are ready to receive it. Go, don't linger, don't wait, don't hesitate, but move now and return to the places from which you came, and let those whom you left behind in their hiding places know that there is nothing to be afraid of, that he is risen, risen indeed."

It is important to realize that the mission is, first of all, a mission to those who are no strangers to us. They know us and, like us, have heard about Jesus but have become discouraged. The mission is always first of all to our own, our family, our friends, those who are an intimate part of our lives. That is not a very comfortable realization. I always find it harder to speak about Jesus to those who know me intimately than to those who have never had to deal with my "peculiar ways of being." Still there lies a great challenge here. Somehow the authenticity of our experience is tested by our parents, our spouses, our children, our brothers and sisters, all those who know us all too well.

Many times we will hear: "Well, that's him again. Well, that's her again. We know what this is all about. We have seen all this excitement before. It will pass...as before." Often there is a lot of truth to this. Why should they trust us when we come running home all excited? Why should they take us seriously? We are not that trustworthy; we are not that different from the rest of our family and friends. Moreover, the world is full of stories, full of rumors, full of preachers and evangelists. There is good reason for some scepticism. Those who didn't go with us to the Eucharist are no better or worse than we are. They have heard the story of Jesus. Some were baptized; some even went to church for a while or for a long time. But then, gradually, the story of Jesus became just a story. Church became obligation, the Eucharist a ritual. Somewhere it all became a sweet or bitter memory. Somewhere something died in them. And why should anyone who knows us well suddenly believe us when we return from the Eucharist?

That is the reason why it is not just the Eucharist, but the *Eucharistic life* that makes the difference. Each day, yes, each moment of the day, there is the pain of our losses and the opportunity to listen to a word that asks us to choose to live these losses as a way to glory. Each day, too, there is the possibility to invite the stranger into our home and to let him break the bread for us. The Eucharistic celebration has summarized for us what our life of faith is all about, and we have to go home to live it as long and as fully as we can. And this is very difficult, because everyone at home knows us so well: our impatience, our jealousies, our resentments, and our many little games. And then there are our broken relationships, our unfulfilled promises, and our unkept commitments. Can we really say that we have met him on the road, have received his body and blood and become living Christs? Everyone at home is ready to test us.

But there is something else. There is a great surprise awaiting the two excited companions who came running to the room where their friends were gathered... eager to tell the news. These friends knew it already! The good news they had to bring was not new after all. Before they even had a chance to tell their story, the eleven and their companions said, "The Lord has indeed risen and has appeared to Simon." It is quite humorous. Here they come running in, out of breath, all excited, only to discover that those who stayed in the city already had heard the news, even though they had not met him on the road or sat at the table with him. Jesus had appeared to Simon, and Simon was a lot more credible than these two disciples who hadn't stayed with them but had gone home thinking that it was all over. Sure, they were glad and eager to hear their story, but they brought just another affirmation that, indeed, he was alive.

There are many ways in which Jesus appears and many ways in which he lets us know that he is alive. What we celebrate in the Eucharist happens in many ways other than we might think. Jesus, who gave us bread already, touched the hearts of others long before he met us on the road. He called someone by her name, and she knew that it was him; he showed his wounds to some, and they knew that it was him. We have our stories to tell, and it is important that we tell them, but they are not the only stories. We have a mission to fulfill and it is good that we are excited about it, but first we have to listen to what others have to say. Then our stories can be told and bring joy.

All of this points to community. The two friends, who were able to speak to each other about their burning hearts, were beginning to enter into a new relationship with one another, a relationship built on the communion they had both experienced. Their communion with Jesus was, indeed, the beginning of community. But only the beginning. They needed to meet the others who also believed that he is risen, who also saw him or heard that he is alive. They needed to listen to their stories, each one different from the others, and to discover the many ways in which Jesus and his Spirit work among his people.

It is so easy to narrow Jesus down to *our* Jesus, to *our* experience of his love, to *our* way of knowing him. But Jesus left us so as to send his Spirit, and his Spirit blows where it wants. The community of faith is the place where many stories about the way of Jesus are being told. These stories can be very different from each other. They might even seem to conflict. But as we keep listening attentively to the Spirit manifesting itself through many people, in words as well as in silence, through confrontation as well as invitation, in gentleness as well as firmness, with tears as well as smiles — then we can gradually discern that we belong together, as one body knitted together by the Spirit of Jesus.

In the Eucharist we are asked to leave the table and go to our friends to discover with them that Jesus is truly alive and calls us together to become a new people – a people of the resurrection.

Here the story of Cleopas and his friend ends. It ends with the two friends telling their story to the eleven and their companions. But the mission does not end here; it has scarcely begun. The telling of the story of what happened on the road and around the table is the beginning of a life of mission, lived all the days of our lives until we see him again face to face.

Forming a community with family and friends, building a body of love, shaping a new people of the resurrection: all of this is not just so that we can live a life protected from the dark forces that dominate our world; it is, rather, to enable us to proclaim together to all people, young and old, white and black, poor and rich, that death does not have the last word, that hope is real and God is alive.

The Eucharist is always mission. The Eucharist that has freed us from our paralyzing sense of loss and revealed to us that the Spirit of Jesus lives within us empowers us to go out into the world and to bring good news to the poor, sight to the blind, liberty to the captives, and to proclaim that God has shown again his favor to all people. But we are not sent out alone; we are sent with our brothers and sisters who also know that Jesus lives within them.

The movement flowing from the Eucharist is the movement from communion to community to ministry. Our experience of communion first sends us to our brothers and sisters to share with them our stories and build with them a body of love. Then, as community, we can move in all directions and reach out to all people.

I am deeply aware of my own tendency to want to go from communion to ministry without forming community. My individualism and desire for personal success ever and again tempt me to do it alone and to claim the task of ministry for myself. But Jesus himself didn't preach and heal alone. Luke, the Evangelist, tells us how he spent the night in communion with God, the morning to form community with the twelve apostles, and the afternoon to go out with them ministering to the crowds. Jesus calls us to the same sequence: from communion to community to ministry. He does not want us to go out alone. He sends us out together, two by two, never by ourselves. And so we can witness as people who belong to a body of faith. We are sent out to teach, to heal, to inspire, and to offer hope to the world — not as the exercise of our unique skill, but as the expression of our faith that all we have to give comes from him who brought us together.

Life lived Eucharistically is always a life of mission. We live in a world groaning under its losses: the merciless wars destroying people and their countries, the hunger and starvation decimating whole populations, crime and violence holding millions of men, women, and children in fear. Cancer and AIDS, cholera, malaria, and many other diseases devastating the bodies of countless people; earthquakes, floods, and traffic disasters . . . it's the story of everyday life filling the newspapers and television screens. It is a world of endless losses, and many, if not most, of our fellow human beings walk with faces downcast on the surface of this planet. They say in some way or another: "Our hope had been . . . but we lost hope."

This is the world we are sent to live in Eucharistically, that is, to live with burning hearts and with open ears and open eyes. It seems an impossible task. What can this small group of people who met him on the road, in the garden, or at the lakeside do in such a dark and violent world? The mystery of God's love is that our burning hearts and our receptive ears and eyes will be able to discover that the One we met in the intimacy of our homes continues to reveal himself to us among the poor, the sick, the hungry, the prisoners, the refugees, and all people who live in fear.

Here we come to realize that mission is not only to go and tell others about the risen Lord, but also to receive that witness from those to whom we are sent. Often mission is thought of exclusively in terms of giving, but true mission is also receiving. If it is true that the Spirit of Jesus blows where it wants, there is no person who cannot give that Spirit. In the long run, mission is possible only when it is as much receiving as giving, as much being cared for as caring. We are sent to the sick, the dying, the handicapped, the prisoners, and the refugees to bring them the good news of the Lord's resurrection. But we will soon be burned out if we cannot receive the Spirit of the Lord from those to whom we are sent.

That Spirit, the Spirit of love, is hidden in their poverty, brokenness, and grief. That is why Jesus said: "Blessed are the poor, the persecuted, and those who mourn." Each time we reach out to them they in turn — whether they are aware of it or not — will bless us with the Spirit of Jesus and so become our ministers. Without this mutuality of giving and receiving, mission and ministry easily become manipulative or violent. When only one gives and the other receives, the giver will soon become an oppressor and the receivers, victims. But when the giver receives and the receiver gives, the circle of love, begun in the community of the disciples, can grow as wide as the world.

It belongs to the essence of the Eucharistic life to make this circle of love grow. Having entered into communion with Jesus and created community with those who know that he is alive, we now can go and join the many lonely travelers and help them discover that they too have the gift of love to share. We are no longer afraid of their sadness and pain, but can ask them simply: "What are you talking about as you walk along the road?" And we will hear stories of immense loneliness, fear, rejection, abandonment, and sadness. We must listen, often for a long time, but there are also opportunities to say with words or simple gestures: "Didn't you know that what you are complaining about can also be lived as a way to something new? Maybe it is impossible to change what has happened to you, but you are still free to choose how to live it."

Not everyone will listen to us and only a few will invite us into their lives to join them at their table. Only seldom will it be possible to offer life-giving bread and truly heal a heart that has been broken. Jesus himself didn't heal everyone, nor change everyone's life. Most people simply don't believe that radical changes are possible and can't give their trust when they meet the strangers. But every time there is a real encounter leading from despair to hope and from bitterness to gratitude, we will see some of the darkness being dispelled and life, once again, breaking through the boundaries of death.

This has been, and continues to be, the experience of those who live a Eucharistic life. They see it as their mission to persistently challenge their fellow travelers to choose for gratitude instead of resentment and for hope instead of despair. And the few times that this challenge is accepted are enough to make their lives worth living. To see a smile breaking through tears is to witness a miracle — the miracle of joy.

Statistically, none of this is very interesting. Those who ask: "How many people did you reach? How many changes did you bring about? How many illnesses did you cure? How much joy did you create?" will always receive disappointing answers. Jesus and his followers did not have great success. The world is still a dark world, full of violence, corruption, oppression, and exploitation. It will likely always be! The question is not: "How soon and how many?" but "Where and when?" Where is the Eucharist being celebrated, where are the people who come together around the table and break bread together, and when does it happen? The world lies in the power of the evil one. The world does not recognize the light that shines in the darkness. It never did; it never will. But there are people who, in the midst of this world, live with the knowledge that he is alive and dwells within us, that he has overcome the power of death and opens the way to glory. Are there people who come together, who come around the table and do what he did, in memory of him? Are there people who keep telling each other the stories of hope and, together, go out to care for their fellow human beings, not pretending to solve all problems, but to bring a smile to a dying man and a little hope to a lonely child?

It is so little, so unspectacular, yes, so hidden, this Eucharistic life, but it is like yeast, like a mustard seed, like a smile on a baby's face. It is what keeps faith, hope and love alive in a world that is constantly on the brink of self-destruction.

The Eucharist, sometimes, is celebrated with great ceremony, in splendid cathedrals and basilicas. But more often it is a "small" event that few people know about. It happens in a living room, a prison cell, an attic – out of sight of the big movements of the world. It happens in secret, without vestments, candles, or incense. It happens with gestures so simple that outsiders don't even know that it takes place. But big or small, festive or hidden, it is the same event, revealing that life is stronger than death and love stronger than fear.

Conclusion

The word "Eucharist" means literally "thanks-giving." A Eucharistic life is one lived in gratitude. The story, which is also our story, of the two friends walking to Emmaus has shown that gratitude is not an obvious attitude toward life. Gratitude needs to be discovered and to be lived with great inner attentiveness. Our losses, our experiences of rejection and abandonment, and our many moments of disillusionment keep pulling us into anger, bitterness, and resentment. When we simply let the "facts" speak, there will always be enough facts to convince us that life, in the end, leads to nothing and that every attempt to beat that fate is only a sign of profound naiveté.

Jesus gave us the Eucharist to enable us to choose gratitude. It is a choice we, ourselves, have to make. Nobody can make it for us. But the Eucharist prompts us to cry out to God for mercy, to listen to the words of Jesus, to invite him into our home, to enter into communion with him and proclaim good news to the world; it opens the possibility of gradually letting go of our many resentments and choosing to be grateful. The Eucharistic celebration keeps inviting us to that attitude. In our daily lives we have countless opportunities to be grateful instead of resentful. At first, we might not recognize these opportunities. Before we fully realized, we have already said: "This is too much for me. I have no choice but to be angry and to let my anger show. Life isn't fair, and I can't act as if it is." However, there is always the voice that, ever and again, suggests that we are blinded by our own understanding and pull ourselves and each other into a hole. It is the voice that calls us "foolish," the voice that asks us to have a completely new look at our lives, a look not from below, where we count our losses, but from above, where God offers us his glory.

Eucharist – thanksgiving – in the end, comes from above. It is the gift that we cannot fabricate for ourselves. It is to be received. It is freely offered and asks to be freely received. That is where the choice is! We can choose to let the stranger continue his journey and so remain a stranger. But we can also invite him into our inner lives, let him touch every part of our being and then transform our resentments into gratitude. We don't have to do this. In fact, most people don't. But as often as we make that choice, everything, even the most trivial things, become new. Our little lives become great – part of the mysterious work of God's salvation. Once that happens, nothing is accidental, casual, or futile any more. Even the most insignificant event speaks the language of faith, hope, and, above all, love. That's the Eucharistic life, the life in which everything becomes a way of saying "Thank you" to him who joined us on the road.